POEMS

by **Dai Blatchford**

Rosie, since these poems would not exist were it not for you I thought that you should have your own personal copy. This is it. You always were and always will be my muse. Thank you for everything.

Dai Poet xxxxxx

M

*Moot*Edition[s]

First published in 2011
by MootEdition[s]
Crwys Farmhouse, Three Crosses, Swansea SA4 3PX

Typeset and printed by Moot Editorial and Design
www.mootideas.co.uk

SECOND EDITION : 2019

10 9 8 7 6 5 4 3 2

Nº

7 /50

This book is a Moot*Edition[s]* publication.

The first edition was unique, hand-bound and presented to the author.
Subsequent printings will be limited but, with luck, in print runs longer than one.

CONTENTS

1. Ice Cream Lover

For a time one summer
I had an ice cream lover
She was colder than ice but also creamy and sweet
We spent many happy hours in her temperature controlled bed
She could be cold and frosty, or warm and creamy
We slept in the biggest bed I have ever seen
With enough room for three
But we never rose to such depths or sank to such heights
Depending on how you look at things.
It is true that she jealously protected her bed territory
With a wall of giant ice cream wafers layered like a palisade.
At certain times she also hung a sign saying 'Keep Out'
On her perimeter wall and I respected her privacy
Merely calling out a regular 'goodnight' at bedtime.

As the days passed I noticed that she began to thaw
And at first I thought this a good thing
I anticipated a more intimate relationship with my ice cream lover.
To my despair this is not what happened.
Instead, one day taking a sneak peek over the biscuit palisade
I noticed the third figure I feared
Had suddenly appeared.
He was tall, tanned and erect
His muscles rippled even though he was lying down
This was an unwelcome development
Something important had changed.

As the days passed the two became close
Then closer still, until
The relationship I feared
Eventually appeared
And my ice cream lover
In time became a 99.

2. Some Things Never Change

Geese are probably not ideally suited
To the profession of lap dancing.
They lack some of the attraction
Of the human female form.
Be that as it is they have the capacity
To move their necks in a certain
Sinuous and sexual way
Capable of stimulating
The jaded businessman and the erring husband.

And so it was that when the Goosey Goosey Club
Opened its doors at the end of our road
Jaded businessmen and erring husbands
Switched their allegiance from the Cuddly Canary Club
In droves. The husbands of the performing geese
Came for a gander but stayed as waiters
Even though they lacked the appendages necessary
To become successful waiters. But in a certain light
And wearing an appropriate outfit they passed for waiters
In a Disney sort of way.

For a month or two the Goosey Goosey Club prospered
Offering relief, at a price,
To jaded businessmen and erring husbands
But one day Gilbert the goose who had started the club
Noticed that his clientele was dwindling, in droves
He took a drive to the other end of our road
Only to see to his horror that someone had opened
The Pink Flamingo Lap Dancing Club with a welter of neon
And a queue stretching around the block
Of jaded businessmen and erring husbands.

3. Feeding Time at the Zoo

It is a sad time, feeding time at the zoo
In a lost land
Where there are many cuts
That grown ups say are for the sake of the economy
And everywhere there are cuts
Why in some places even corners are being cut.
In the zoo many of these cuts are prime cuts
Taken from smaller creatures
Where they are inventively used
To feed the larger and therefore more important ones.
It is a sad time, feeding time at the zoo

Sometimes rare deer are
Ushered into the compounds
Usually reserved for the big cats
The valuable big cats that have grown fat and lazy
For they are institutionalised and unused
To chasing their meat.
Sad eyed zookeepers are forced
To slaughter the deer and serve them up
On silver platters to the now only quite fat cats.
It is a sad time, feeding time at the zoo

The accountant who manages the zoo
Regularly points out that
This is not a sustainable policy
And that, currently the zoo is even
Running out of seals on which to feed the polar bears.
And he also wonders what will happen
When they are reduced to slaughtering
The contents of the petting zoo
Will that be several cuts too far?
And where will the children play?
It looks like there is no alternative
And a sad time will be had by all
When it is feeding time at the zoo.

4. Lost Love Poem

At night
I lie awake
Hugging my pillow
Wishing it were you.

I hear that
At night
You too lie awake
Hugging another man's pillow
I hope he will be good to you.

5. The Last of the Hooded Grebes

Hooded grebes are
An endangered species
They sit on the red list
Soon there may be no more hooded grebes
I felt I should bring this to your attention
Hoping that the facts may encourage you to care
But I am not that hopeful.
So what is this poem about?
Well, it is about 15 lines
Including the title
Which is of course optional
And

Like poems of this
Or any other age
Written by a dreamer
not by a sage.

6. Fragments from Meandering Nature Poems

Snake in the Grass

Once I saw a snake in the grass
It was quite a fat snake
I suppose in snake terms
It would qualify as obese.
It had caught its fat, snaky neck
In some wire and was pulling
With all its might to get free
Stretching and stretching
Its snaky body in a snaky panic.
All I could think of was this.
I wondered whether in its snaky mind
It was thinking, "What doesn't kill me
Can only make me longer?'

Do Bears Fit in the Woods?

Brown bears are getting lazy
They are no longer the lean mean
Brown browsers of legend
But are snacking on burgers, crisps and pizzas
Such behaviour would, of course,
Meet with the full approval
Of the legendary Yogi Bear and his sidekick
Boo Boo from whom no pickernick basket was ever safe.
But there is a serious issue here
Fat bears simply do not look right
Resembling overweight hairy humans
And such bears no longer fit in the woods.

7. Bigfoot Boogie

Bigfoot wherever he may be
Has become fascinated with
Programmes about dance.
So entranced by television dance
Is the mythical Sasquatch
That he has joined a dancing school.

Every Wednesday at around four pm
He rides the bus to the Dance School
Just off Main Street where he takes instruction
In various dance styles.
Because of his size and the fact that he doesn't exist
He finds difficulty in getting partners.

His solution is to dance alone
And his preferred style of music
Is piano boogie played loud
To which he boogies like
A thing possessed until finally exhausted
He catches the bus home to a forest bristling with hunters.

At High Schools and Colleges all over America
The kids are happily dancing the Bigfoot Boogie
And demonstrating for the right of mythical creatures
Whatever they may be, wherever they may dance
To live in peace and to dance their cares away
For this God blesses America.

8. The Spear Carrier's Apprentice

My name is Kit Marlowe and
I am the spear-carrier's apprentice.
It is a lowly task but
I carry it out with Gusto
Who, incidentally is
My best friend.
I believe him to be Italian.
He is certainly quite dark
And frequently smells of Garlic
Who, incidentally is
My black cat.
I believe him to be
Neutered. He is certainly quite dark
And frequently smells of mice
These he brings me as corpses
As I strut my stuff off stage.
One day I shall make the leap (Tights willing)
To spear carrier number one
Then I'll show the groundlings
How a spear should be carried.

With great élan and style
On my face a winning smile
And on my back a sign that
Says he never married.

9. Dead Cool in Deptford

My name is Kit Marlowe and
You may remember me
From poems such as
The Spear Carrier's Apprentice.
Life has changed for me
And I am beginning to make waves
In this theatrical business.
There are those who say
That I am also becoming a big cheese
In the underhand world of spying
You may think that but I couldn't
Possibly comment. Both Gusto and Garlic
Are still with me and I love them both.
I no longer carry spears around
Rickety stages. I now use my quill
To do the talking for me.
My clothes are flamboyant
As befits my personality
And let's face it theatre types
Are expected to be a little
Outgoing. Will and I often
Take drink in Eleanor Bull's
It reminds me of the theatre there
And it throngs with the low life types
Who have always attracted me.
Gusto and Garlic never accompany me
Especially when I have a thirst to satisfy
So I have acquired some new companions
Ingram, Skeres and Poley
None of these is very colourful
Nor at all theatrical
If you know what I mean
But they seem to find me dead cool
In Deptford and I've always loved
Performing in public.

10. Dead in Deptford

My name is Kit Marlowe and
I am now officially dead.
You may think it strange
That others think the way others think
Otherwise. Some say that I am in thrall to
Walsingham. Some say that I am quartered abroad
Venice being the usual favourite.
You might think that but I couldn't
Possibly comment. Though I will say
And this may be a hidden clue
That I am definitely not writing
Anybody else's plays for them
And I think you know who I mean.
That particular "upstart crow" can manage
Very well on his own and as I have said
I am officially dead. Unfortunately for some
That is simply not enough so they have
Carefully constructed what will come to be called
Conspiracy theories to explain, to the satisfaction of all
The small death of England's greatest poet, playwright
And performer.

This is what really happened
I was drinking at Eleanor Bull's house with my
Three new friends Frizer, Skeres and Poley
Claret of course and plenty of it.
There was no argument about the bill
We were just very, very drunk.
It was Frizer who made an insulting remark
I told him to withdraw but he lunged at me
Piercing my eye with his dagger.
My death scene following this underhand attack
Was exquisitely played out.
It was my finest public performance.
Officially that was the end
Of England's greatest poet, playwright and performer.
I died as I had lived with great élan and style
Cut down in my prime. Though there were still those
Who questioned events? And through it all the Widow Bull
Maintained an undignified silence.

11. The Poet Passes

Not with a clamour of brass and wind
Not with a clashing storm and lashing rain
Not with a blizzard of hopeless dreams
But with a vestigial dignity and some silence
Not with a clang
But with a whimper.

12. The Trouble with Poems

Tricky chaps, poems.
You can never trust a poem
Unless you have known it for a long time.
Some of them are OK
They can be trusted
Some poems won't let you down.
Others are trouble from the off
I'm naming no names
But I think you know who you are
Those that began with loads of promise
But then took their own course
A strong line with such poems is required
Discipline and where appropriate
tough love to correct the silent rebellion
Some, poems like this one simply never................

13. A Man of My Age (In memoriam: Roy Dymond)

When I heard about your trouble
I found it difficult to accept
You had always seemed so alive
And the disease that was killing you
Was a new one on me
The effect of such sad news
Was to galvanise me
Into a form of action.
I began to live
Like a man possessed
I ate in a more abandoned manner
Especially those things held to be dangerous
For a man of my age.
I drank even more heavily
Heartily enjoying every drunken moment
Though pausing regularly
To toast you in your trouble.

Now that you are gone
I have returned to my old ways.
My intake of dangerous substances
Has been greatly reduced
I take regular exercise
But still lie awake at night, wondering
Whether the shadow on the landing
Really carries a scythe over his shoulder.

14. Hamlet

As a child I was solitary
And thoughtful.
My mother thought I needed
A companion
So she introduced me to the neighbourhood rabbit.
It too was solitary and thoughtful.
It was a black rabbit
That she, in her humour
Had nicknamed Hamlet
It was the only joke
Of my childhood.

15. Curtains

Daily drawing back curtains
Is an act of faith
Implicit in which is the belief
That outside might just improve
On the unremarkable inside.
Daily I draw back curtains
And intend to continue
With this brave though ultimately
Futile practice.

On one of these endless days
Curtains, probably made of blue velvet
And operated by a clever electrical device
Will finally be drawn
Around me

16. The Cost of DIY

I saw a man once
Working on a roof
And as he worked
The sound of his hammer
Created a sharp echo
When he fell the sharp echo
Disappeared
To be replaced by the much duller sound
Of a body hurtling
Into the newly laid drive
Of a newly bought home.

17. Street Life – Soft Shoe Shuffle

The holy driven martyr
Shuffles through Sunday streets.
Street life abounds
As he shuffles softly
Through the centuries.

Perhaps he does not appear
Modern enough to
Attract attention
Perhaps his sad, old face
Speaks of space
Behind the stars
Holding only horrors
For mankind.

Whatever the reason
Jude's pale Galilean
Has much time to reflect
As he shuffles through
Sunday streets.

18. Ancient Forces

As a child I was approached
By an old gypsy woman
She was persistent
In her attempts
To sell me
A lucky shell.

As a smart kid
I rudely refused to buy
Knowing full well
Where to find
Thousands of such shells
On nearby beaches.

But long after our chance meeting
I spent nights of terror
Wondering, as even smart kids do
Whether I had challenged
Ancient forces.

19. The Adman Cometh

If I ever do reinvent the wheel
I shall make it square
Functionally useless, perhaps
But rather quaint
And with an ambitious marketing budget
A surefire winner.

20. Poetry by Numbers

It is clear to me
That poetry and numbers
Do not mix.
I am prepared to acknowledge
The sonnet form
With its patronising nod
To the world of mathematics
Though in truth
I find it constricting.

Poetry should eschew restrictions
And salmon like, defy the odds
Challenging every rock and pool
As it strives to reach
The water gods.

21. Ready for Theatre

After the audition
I was sure
I'd got the part
But the only thing
They had for me
Was this artificial heart.

22. Pigeons

I have recently developed
A fear of tripping over pigeons.
This is obsessive behaviour
Of a feathery kind.

My ordered life has changed
No longer do I linger in parks
On sunny days for fear
Of packs of roosting pigeons.

I tend to skirt wooded areas
Ever alert to the threat of aerial attack
And remain constantly fearful
Of tripping over earthbound pigeons
Cruelly lying in wait
For a victim of obsessive behaviour.

23. Cold Messiah – A Poem for Christmas

A cold collation
They had of it
But then it was January
And no landlord
Would waste leftover turkey.

The kings, if kings they were
Had taken the bus
And a cold coming they had of it.
The infant Jesus lay
Quietly swaddled, but cold.

After all this was January
And ice had formed
Of course this was not
Bethlehem
But a much colder place
And the infant Jesus
A much colder Messiah.

24. An Hour Later he Died

An hour later he died
The child of innocence
And during the hour
Unconnected people talked
Not of his death
But of its cause

The child of innocence
Heard not those people
Nor knew the cause
He knew he was hungry
And knowing, he died

25. Haiku

Suddenly this summer
Sun on a leaf
Through sad clouds
Briefly clearing.

26. Lingerie Poem

I wonder whether
Esther ever
Wears a Freudian slip

27. Too Much to Lose

I gave her my mackerel
But really she wanted my sole

28. Barbecue Poem (1)

Often I feel
Like a ghost at a barbecue
Wearing a clean white shirt
Quietly affecting nonchalance
As the ketchup starts to squirt

29. Barbecue Poem (2)

She said, "This food is awful
Black, burned and oozing red"
I said, "I have done my best"
As we raked over the embers
Of a dying relationship.

30. A Simple Death

The jumping man
Stood on the ledge
His leading foot
Quite near the edge
"My life no longer
Works" he said
"I'll be much happier
When I'm dead."

A crowd had gathered
Far below
All come to see
The suicide show

From the crowd
A single voice
"You needn't jump
You have a choice."
"I have a choice" the
Man replied
He simply jumped
And simply died.